PASSENGER PIGEON

For a free color catalog describing Gareth Stevens Publishing's list of high-quality books and multimedia programs, call 1-800-542-2595 (USA) or 1-800-461-9120 (Canada). Gareth Stevens Publishing's Fax: (414) 225-0377. See our catalog, too, on the World Wide Web: http://gsinc.com

Library of Congress Cataloging-in-Publication Data

Coleman, Graham, 1963-
    Passenger pigeon / by Graham Coleman ; illustrated by Tony Gibbons.
      p. cm. — (The extinct species collection)
    Includes index.
    Summary: Describes what is known of the history and habits of the North American bird that once numbered in the millions before becoming extinct in the early twentieth century.
    ISBN 0-8368-1594-7 (lib. bdg.)
    1. Passenger pigeon—Juvenile literature. 2. Extinct birds—North America—Juvenile literature. [1. Passenger pigeon. 2. Pigeons. 3. Extinct animals.]
I. Gibbons, Tony, ill. II. Title. III. Series.
QL696.C63C64   1996
598.6′5—dc20
                                            96-4996

First published in North America in 1996 by
Gareth Stevens Publishing
1555 North RiverCenter Drive, Suite 201
Milwaukee, WI 53212 USA

This U.S. edition © 1996 by Gareth Stevens, Inc. Created with original © 1995 by Quartz Editorial Services, 112 Station Road, Edgware HA8 7AQ U.K. under the title *The Passenger Pigeon*.

Additional artwork by Clare Heronneau

U.S. Editors: Barbara J. Behm, Mary Dykstra

Printed in Mexico

1 2 3 4 5 6 7 8 9 99 98 97 96

the
EXTINCT
SPECIES
collection

PASSENGER PIGEON

by Graham Coleman
Illustrated by Tony Gibbons

Gareth Stevens Publishing
MILWAUKEE

Contents

Meet the
passenger pigeon

Huge flocks of **passenger pigeons** once filled the skies over North America. There were sometimes several million of them in just one flock. At one time, the **passenger pigeon** was thought to be the most plentiful bird in the world.

It would be hard to imagine a less likely candidate for extinction. In fact, around 1860, scientists estimated there were between 5 and 10 billion **passenger pigeons** in existence!

Yet amazingly, within about fifty years, this once common bird had vanished from the face of the Earth.

What were **passenger pigeons** like? How fast could they fly? Why did their numbers decrease so quickly? How did they become extinct? Read on and find out all about **passenger pigeons** and their tragic disappearance.

Fast flier

Known by scientists as *Ectopistes migratorius* (EC-TOE-PIS-TEES MY-GRA-TOR-EE-US), the **passenger pigeon** was an attractive, multicolored bird. It had a gray-blue head, pink breast, and red legs. Its wings — each with a span of about 8 inches (20 centimeters) — were various shades of brown, gray, and white.

From head to tail, the males grew to a length of about 16 inches (40 cm) — much bigger than the common pigeons or rock doves of today. The female **passenger pigeons** were smaller than the males and less brightly colored, as were the young birds.

The **passenger pigeon**'s body was designed for speed. It had a streamlined body, powerful breast muscles, and pointed wings. Its long tail extended beyond its body about 8 inches (20 cm).

Some experts estimate this bird could fly as fast as 60 miles (96 kilometers) per hour — over the speed limit for cars in many places. People who saw them fly often remarked how elegant these birds looked as they sped overhead.

However, in spite of their great speed, they were easy prey for hunters.

Passenger pigeons were almost always in flight, searching for new nesting sites and feeding grounds.

With their excellent vision, **passenger pigeons** were able to spot suitable nesting and feeding sites from high in the sky. Then, if one bird swooped, the others would follow. These birds were highly social and could not survive without the flock.

Flocks of **passenger pigeons** usually made a deafening racket. Observers reported they made different sounds at different times — a strange croaking when they were building nests; a bell-like sound when they were mating; and a variety of shrieks, warbles, and coos for unknown reasons.

What noisy birds they must have been — especially in such large numbers!

North American native

The **passenger pigeon** was an all-American bird, living only in the United States. Some experts believe more than a quarter of all birds in this part of the world were **passenger pigeons**.

Most of the birds inhabited deciduous forests, ranging as far north as the border with Canada.

Passenger pigeons also filled the skies far into the southern states. Their homeland covered a great part of North America.

Everywhere they went in their vast numbers, **passenger pigeons** would leave their mark, as pictured in this illustration. The ground would be full of their droppings as well as with tree branches broken by their weight.

If you had lived 150 years ago, you would have seen thousands of **passenger pigeons** resting in trees or flying in huge flocks in the sky.

Turn the page to get an idea of what it must have been like to see a flock of **passenger pigeons**, possibly about 1 mile (1.6 km) wide, passing overhead.

8

9

On the move

Like the young man in this illustration, people were amazed when **passenger pigeon** flocks flew overhead. There must have been a sound like one continuous peal of thunder. One expert estimated that a single flock could have been as long as 320 miles (510 km).

When the famous nineteenth-century American ornithologist and artist John James Audubon saw a great flock of **passenger pigeons** overhead, he said the "light of (the) noonday sun was obscured as by an eclipse." In other words, there were so many of the birds in such a dense mass that they blocked the sunlight. The sky seemed to grow dark, even though it was the middle of the day!

Sometimes, however, the flocks decreased in size. This happened when food was not plentiful. The **passenger pigeons** would then spread out to look for food.

Flocks would suddenly descend when they spotted what looked like a good feeding area. Then they would circle around it in a formation that looked like a "rolling cylinder," according to one observer. After the **passenger pigeons** had eaten most of the food available there, they would move on.

Settling

Like the pair shown *below*, many of the birds were busy building nests. The process took about four days, and the timing was critical.

One clear May morning, about 150 years ago, the trees near a Michigan river were heavy with **passenger pigeons**. The birds were sitting in pairs, "chatting" to one another in their own language of calls. This nesting site was about 20 miles (32 km) long, although some might even have been bigger, perhaps twice that size.

As soon as the nest-building was complete, each female laid a single egg. The parents then took turns, night and day, guarding the newly built nest and egg.

12

down

One of the pair would go off to feed, while the other stayed behind. This routine lasted a full twelve days, until the egg began to hatch.

Both parents fed their baby bird seeds, worms, and a special milky substance that was regurgitated from the adult's stomach, or crop.

The chick that eventually emerged was small and plump. The young bird did not look very much like its parents at first. It could not yet fly and had to rely entirely on the two parent birds for food.

Before long, the fledgling bird was ready to leave the nest and was forced out by its parents. It had to learn to care for itself and had to find a mate and build a nest.

Victims of guns

Bang! Bang! Bang! The noise was deafening as large groups of men took aim and shot their guns. But it wasn't just the sound of guns going off at regular intervals that was so disturbing. This was nothing compared with the loud warning cries of innumerable, desperate **passenger pigeons** as they fluttered around, utterly panic-stricken. These poor creatures did not stand a chance.

Hunters also used a variety of traps to catch the birds, including large, sturdy nets. In this way, millions of birds were caught in a single day. These **passenger pigeon** hunts were usually major kills.

But not all birds were killed outright. Some were trapped and kept alive for later release at events where they would be shot for sport.

The slaughter of **passenger pigeons** continued year after year, so that their flocks quickly became severely depleted.

A number of theories have been suggested to explain the eventual disappearance of the **passenger pigeon**. Some experts have suggested that disease was to blame. Others speculate that there was a shortage of suitable food for the birds.

However, most agree that human beings were undoubtedly to blame, having brought about the extinction of the **passenger pigeon** through hunting. Further, some sources say that the last surviving wild **passenger pigeon** was shot not by a man, but by a child.

and traps

Put to use

Passenger pigeons reproduced quickly in the wild. Because of their abundance and easy capture, they were often found on the dinner table. They were an inexpensive source of food for humans.

The younger the bird, the more tender the meat. And almost anyone could afford a tougher, older **passenger pigeon** for dinner, either served roasted or baked in a pie.

It may be hard to imagine eating such an attractive bird, but **passenger pigeons** were commonly found in nineteenth-century American kitchens. Of course, they were not bred on farms for food. People simply shot them in the wild and brought them home for the family supper. For large banquets, **passenger pigeons** were shot by the hundreds.

These birds were put to many other uses, too. Strangely, some nineteenth-century people believed that certain parts of the **passenger pigeon** — its stomach and even its droppings, for example — could cure certain illnesses or bring down a fever.

Today, thankfully, the world no longer relies on **passenger pigeon** medicine!

Every part of the **passenger pigeon** was used in some way. Its down, for example, provided soft stuffing for pillows and cushions. In the course of a day, some people probably dined on a **passenger pigeon**, sat on a **passenger pigeon** cushion, and then went to sleep under a quilt stuffed with the feathers of the unfortunate birds of this species.

Menu

Vegetable soup

Passenger pigeon pie

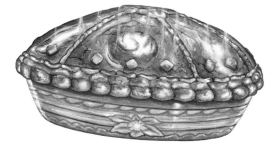

Baked potatoes

Apple flan

Martha's

By the end of the nineteenth century, so many millions of **passenger pigeons** had been massacred that they had nearly vanished from the planet.

The **passenger pigeon**, once so common that flocks completely blocked the sun, had become a rare sight. The last sighting in the wild was in 1900. Like so many others, this final bird was shot and killed. Its remains can now be seen in the Ohio State Museum.

A few **passenger pigeons** had been captured and taken to zoos, but they did not respond well to captivity and often failed to breed. In 1909, only three **passenger pigeons** remained, two males and one female. By the next year, only the female survived. She was born in captivity at the Cincinnati Zoological Gardens and named Martha by the zookeepers.

Since it was well known that Martha was the last of her species, she became a celebrity. Many people came to see this rare bird.

But on September 1, 1914, Martha died. It was reported she was twenty-nine years old at the time. It's easy to imagine how devastated her keeper and many others must have been when she died.

Martha's body was frozen in a block of ice and taken to the Smithsonian Institution in Washington, D.C., where the bird was stuffed and put on display. Martha can still be seen there today. Although long dead, Martha is still admired by visitors to the museum's natural history collection.

final hour

Pigeons of

Several other types of pigeons have become extinct, including the **pigeon hollandaise**, or Dutch pigeon, shown *below*. It was given this name by the ornithologist P. Sonnerat in the eighteenth century because its coloring reminded him of the Dutch flag. It was not a native of the Netherlands, however, but was fairly common at one time on the island of Mauritius in the Indian Ocean.

It was hunted by people for its meat.

Another extinct pigeon is the **Choiseul pigeon**, *above*, notable for its attractive crest. It lived only on the Pacific Ocean island of Choiseul in the Solomon Islands. This pigeon died out when much of its habitat was destroyed to make way for coconut plantations. When cats were brought to the island, they often caught and ate these pigeons. No sightings of this bird have been reported since the early 1940s.

the past

The **Bonin wood pigeon**, *below*, lived on a small group of islands south of Japan, known as the Bonins. A **Bonin wood pigeon** was last spotted in 1889 and is now believed to be extinct. As its name suggests, this pigeon was found in wooded areas where it lived on seeds and nuts. It was a colorful, large bird, growing to a length of 18 inches (46 cm). It died out when the islands' forests were cut down to make room for settlers.

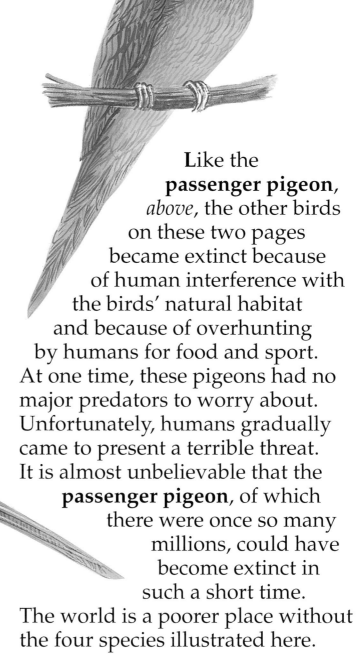

Like the **passenger pigeon**, *above*, the other birds on these two pages became extinct because of human interference with the birds' natural habitat and because of overhunting by humans for food and sport. At one time, these pigeons had no major predators to worry about. Unfortunately, humans gradually came to present a terrible threat. It is almost unbelievable that the **passenger pigeon**, of which there were once so many millions, could have become extinct in such a short time. The world is a poorer place without the four species illustrated here.

Passenger

A great deal is known about the **passenger pigeon**'s behaviors and appearance from written accounts during the time when millions of them flew in the North American skies.

Droppings galore

One ornithologist described the ground under the trees where **passenger pigeons** slept as always "entirely covered with their dung, which lay in great heaps." In fact, when a particular nesting site was visited by a researcher, droppings fell so thickly that the visitor thought, at first, that it was snowing hard!

Big eaters

The American ornithologist Alexander Wilson observed that, on average, a single **passenger pigeon** probably ate about one cup of seeds, berries, fruits, nuts, worms, and insects every day.

Another observation made was that if the birds spotted something that looked tasty, they would regurgitate their previous meal to make room for the new food.

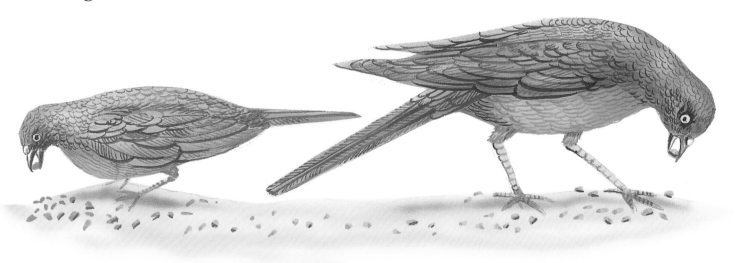

pigeon data

Stool pigeon

Humans were very cruel to the **passenger pigeon**. Not only did men shoot these birds in huge numbers for sport and food, they sewed the eyes of live birds shut and then attached the birds to posts that were known as "stools." The terrified birds flapped their wings, attracting other pigeons that were then caught in nets.

Single eggs

The female laid one egg at a time. It was white and measured about 1.5 inches (38 millimeters) long — about the same size as today's common pigeon's egg. But no one is sure how many times each year the female **passenger pigeons** laid their eggs. The parents looked after the fledgling, or young bird, for just two weeks. After that, it was left to survive on its own.

Glossary

crop — part of a bird's gullet, the passage that leads to the stomach.

deciduous forests — forests of trees that shed their leaves in winter.

dung — the excrement, or droppings, of an animal.

eclipse — when the sun and the moon line up in the sky, so that one blocks, or *eclipses*, the other.

extinct — the state or condition of no longer existing.

fledgling — a young bird that is learning to fly.

flock — a group of birds or mammals gathered together.

ornithologist — a person who is an expert on birds.

regurgitate — when birds or other animals bring food back up into their mouths after swallowing.

reproduce — to produce offspring.

stool pigeon — in history, a passenger pigeon that was cruelly attached to a post, known as a stool, so that the bird's flutterings would attract other pigeons.

Index